READ ON YOUR OWN BOOK 30

MW01706849

A Home for Fox

by Lada Josefa Kratky
illustrated by Francisco X. Mora

NATIONAL GEOGRAPHIC
School Publishing

"Mole, look up," said Fox. "I want to have a home up there."

“Not me, Fox,” said Mole. “I do not like to go up.” But Fox did not give up.

"Look, Mole," said Fox.
"He put a rope up there.
We can go up on the rope."

"Come with me, Mole," said Fox. "Let us see what we can find up there."

"Mole, Mole, see me go up!" said Fox. Fox and Mole did go up and up.

But Mole let go. Paf! Mole made a hole. "This hole is a home for me," said Mole.

But Fox got to the top.
He put a home up there.
Can you see him there?